OLYSLAGER AUTO LIBRARY

Half-Tracks

compiled by the OLYSLAGER ORGANISATION

edited by Bart H. Vanderveen

FREDERICK WARNE & Co Ltd
London and New York

Library of Congress Catalog Card Number 74–91868

ISBN 0 7232 1265 1

Filmset by Keyspools Ltd, Golborne, Lancs,
Printed in Great Britain by C. Tinling & Co. Ltd, Prescot

INTRODUCTION

Although half-track vehicles played a prominent part in the second World War when they were employed by most of the belligerent powers, very few were produced after 1945. This was due partly to the availability of large quantities of vehicles left over from the war, which more than satisfied the military needs of the countries who wanted them, and partly to the development of multi-wheeled vehicles with high-floatation tyres and sophisticated fully tracked vehicles which made the half-track principle obsolete.

Before the advent of low-pressure large-section pneumatic tyres, the half-track design was used because it was the only way of carrying heavy loads over soft ground and snow, without going to the expense of operating full-track machines with their inherent problems of intricate steering/braking mechanisms and high operating costs.

Two basic types of half-tracks emerged. One was the type where track bogies replaced a single-wheeled axle (or tandem axles), the other where most of the vehicle's weight rested on long tracks, and two wheels (or one) were added mainly for steering purposes. The former was purely a hybrid machine. Although it performed reasonably well it tended to combine the shortcomings rather than the advantages of both the wheeled and tracked cross-country vehicle. The other type was basically more like a fully tracked vehicle fitted with a pair of wheels to facilitate steering on roads. For slight turns at speed the steering mechanism would not affect the track drive but the tracks would follow the wheels and only for sharp turns the tracks would be made to 'skid' by actuating the brake-controlled differential. The German *Zgkw* tractors of World War II are good examples of this system.

In this pictorial review of semi-track vehicles we have endeavoured to present typical examples of most of the types produced in various countries, together with some of the many 'odd balls' – such as half-track motor cycles and four-track trucks. Some types are still in use, notably American products of World War II which, in spite of certain shortcomings, still fill a need in several military and civilian applications.

Piet Olyslager MSIA MSAE KIVI

3A

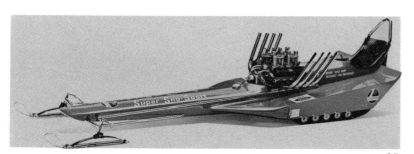

3B

3A: 1910 experimental petrol-engined Holt Caterpillar.
3B: 1970 Ford-engined 150-mph Rupp snowmobile dragster.

The earliest half-track vehicles were produced in the USA soon after the turn of the century. The machines were designed for agricultural use but the military authorities soon showed an interest in their cross-country ability which was very much better than that of contemporary wheeled tractors. Early in World War I the British had acquired and tested specimens of the Bullock Creeping Grip, the Holt Caterpillar and the Killen-Strait (which was later fitted with a Delaunay-Belleville armoured car body), and subsequently acquired over 1500 Holts for use as artillery tractors. The Russians selected the Lombard and during 1917–18 used them for a variety of military purposes such as moving heavy guns and towing trailer trains loaded with ammunition and other supplies. The Red Army also employed Holt Caterpillars.

5B

5A

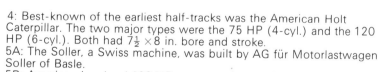

4: Best-known of the earliest half-tracks was the American Holt Caterpillar. The two major types were the 75 HP (4-cyl.) and the 120 HP (6-cyl.). Both had $7\frac{1}{2} \times 8$ in. bore and stroke.
5A: The Soller, a Swiss machine, was built by AG für Motorlastwagen Soller of Basle.
5B: American Lombard 100 HP tractor under test. Note position of tracks on inside of chassis frame. Some had skis at front.
5C: American Killen-Strait three-track agricultural tractor. Tested in 1915 by the British Landships (tanks) committee. In 1917 commercial release by Austin Motor Co. who called it 'Austin Culti-tractor', Model No. 3.

5C

HOLT CONVERSIONS

In addition to their own half-track Caterpillar tractors Holt also produced tracked bogie units for conversion of conventional wheeled vehicles into half-tracks. They were used on various makes of trucks, including FWD, Garford, Jeffery, Nash and Packard and were particularly successful on the FWD Model B and the Jeffery/Nash 'Quad' because these trucks were originally provided with four-wheel drive, and after conversion became the first half-track vehicles with driven front axle. These half-track bogies were similar in design to those of the heavy Holt Caterpillar tractors, but smaller and consequently much lighter.

7A

6: A Garford Model 64 truck of the US Army, converted into a half-track by the Holt Mfg Co., ready for shipment at the Holt factory. In the background can be seen some of the firm's large 120 HP 6-cyl. Caterpillar tractors.

7A: One of the first half-tracks with driven front axle: Jeffery/Nash 'Quad' converted by Holt. Jeffery (Nash from 1917) was one of the largest military truck producers in World War I.

7B: FWD Model B Balloon Winch truck with Holt half-track attachments, 1918.

7C: Packard Model 3D with Holt Caterpillar conversion. Conventional Packard trucks, together with Peerless and Pierce-Arrow, were extensively used by the British Army on the Western front.

7B

7C

In France, the Société des Automobiles Delahaye during 1918 introduced tracked bogies, not unlike those of the American Holt company, for use on their own and other military vehicles. The attachment, called *Chenille Delahaye*, fitted on to the vehicle's rear axle and the drive was taken to the rear sprocket of the bogie by means of a chain. The track bogies, which weighed about half a ton each, could be removed and replaced by road wheels, or vice versa, by six men in about 15 minutes. The front wheel of the bogie was an idler wheel and was adjustable to maintain correct track tension. At the top was a track return support skid, at the bottom the bogie rested on the track by means of three rollers.

DELAHAYE CONVERSIONS

9A

9B

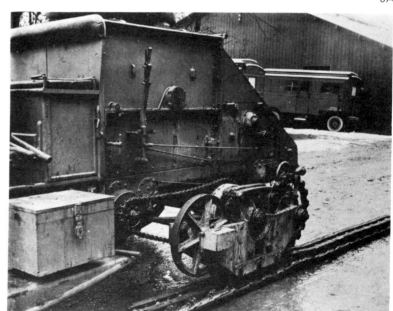
9C

8: The complete *Chenille Delahaye* (Delahaye track) bogie as fitted on a French Saurer truck, clearly showing the layout of the design and the truck's own chain rear axle final drive. The attachments were very heavy and featured dry pin metal track links.
9A: Latil Model TAR heavy four-wheel drive artillery tractor fitted with four Delahaye tracked bogies thus becoming a 'four-track' or 'twin half-track' (as opposed to a 'full-track' in the accepted sense of the word). It was reported, not surprisingly, that steering proved extremely difficult.
9B: Delahaye half-track balloon winch truck of 1918.
9C: The track 'unfolded' showing drive sprocket, idler wheel and track return support skid.

EARLY GERMAN DESIGNS

In 1915/16 the German engineer Hugo E. Bremer designed some cross-country vehicles which were known as *Bremerwagen*.

These vehicles, including an armoured version, were not successful and development was stopped in April 1917. The Daimler Motoren Gesellschaft of Marienfelde, Berlin, however, set out to improve the design and subsequently introduced the *Marienwagen*. Various half- and four-track types were produced and tested during 1916–18.

The Benz-Bräuer-*Kraftprotze* was the result of various experiments with half-track vehicles by Benz in Gaggenau, starting in 1917. A batch of 200 was ordered by the German Army in 1918, but only 50 were completed by the end of the war and these were scrapped, in compliance with the Treaty of Versailles.

11A

11B

11C

10: *Bremerwagen:* experimental four-track conversion of Daimler 45 HP 4-ton truck. German military authorities ordered 20 in 1916. Weight: 6.6 tons. Payload: 2.5 tons. Speed: 12 km/h (roads), 6 km/h (cross-country).

11A: Benz-Bräuer-*Kraftprotze* had twin rear wheels; outer ones with track bogies could be lifted off the ground for normal operation.

28/42 HP production model shown. Also tried on a conventional Benz truck.

11B: *Bremer-Überland-(Sturm) Panzerwagen* (Bremer overland (assault) armoured car).

11C: Daimler *Marienwagen II* (1918), an improvement over the *Bremerwagen,* with heavier track bogies.

The earliest half-track vehicles, most of which were basically agricultural machines, were heavy, cumbersome and slow. This changed during the early 1920s when the Kégresse system was introduced in France. This system comprised continuous rubber bands on light bogies and had first been evolved by Adolphe Kégresse in 1910/11 when he was Technical Manager of the Imperial garages in Russia. He had subsequently converted the Packard and Rolls-Royce cars of Czar Nicholas II for improved performance over snow. Austin armoured cars were also thus converted. Following the Revolution he returned to his native France where industrialists M. Hinstin and André Citroën became interested.

In 1921 the first *Autochenille* appeared and performed very successfully in trials in the French Alps and the Sahara. Soon the system was also produced in other countries.

12: The first Citroën-Kégresse car completed and fitted with bodywork and mudguards. Various types were subsequently developed for civilian and military purposes, including armoured versions.

13A: André Citroën, Dutch by origin, in his first *Autochenille* of 1921. The Kégresse-Hinstin bogies, as can be seen, pivotted on the fixed rear driving axle. For snow trials in the Chamonix area, skis were used underneath the front wheels. Basically it was a contemporary Citroën 10 CV Model B2 car.

13B: Early Citroën-Kégresse half-track with touring car bodywork. Note the extra cooling air louvres in the bonnet (hood) and the clever design of the bogies.

13C: The very first Kégresse half-tracks were conversions of Rolls-Royce and Packard cars in pre-Revolution Russia. Shown here is a Packard, captured by the Germans in World War I.

13D: Close-up of first Kégresse-Hinstin bogie.

KÉGRESSE AUTOCHENILLE

13A

13B

13C

13D

14A: Two very early Citroën-Kégresse *Autochenille* half-tracks during snow trials in the French Alps. Skis for the front axle are carried on the back.

14B: The first crossing of the Sahara desert by motor vehicles was accomplished in 1922–23 using five Citroën-Kégresse vehicles. This is one of them. Note the additional radiator core (both sides) and the badly worn and damaged rubber track. The 3600-km trip took from 18th Dec. to 7th Jan.

14C: Citroën 10 HP *Autochenille* of the 'Black Expedition' giving an impressive show of its 'fordability'. This Central African expedition was, like the first Sahara crossing, directed by Georges-Marie Haardt and Louis Audouin-Dubreuil.

14D: Three of the eight *Autochenilles* of the 'Black Expedition' each towing a two-wheel trailer loaded with spare parts and equipment. The expedition crossed the whole of Africa, from Algeria to the Cape, between Nov. 1924 and July 1925.

14A

14B

14C

14D

15A: The British Crossley-Kégresse 25-cwt chassis, numbers of which were used by the British Army with GS or staff/command car bodywork. The first Crossley-Kégresse, a 40—45 HP model, made its appearance in Oct. 1924.

15B: This heavier type of Crossley-Kégresse was tested by the British Army circa 1925 as a gun tractor and 30-cwt load carrier.

15C: The other British vehicle using Kégresse half-track bogies was the Burford. Shown is the field artillery tractor version of 1926. It weighed just over 3½ tons and had a Burford 4-cyl. 28.8 HP engine. Speed was 15—20 mph on the road, up to 10 mph across country. Load capacity was 30 cwt.

15D: In Italy the Kégresse system was used by Alfa-Romeo for this experimental tractor which could be driven in either direction. To this end there were two driver's seats and two sets of pedals. The steering column was an upright post with two vertical steering wheels.

15A

15B

15C

15D

KÉGRESSE DEVELOPMENTS

The Kégresse system with endless rubber bands was a success from the start and there was soon a demand for a heavier version. A new bogie was then developed and this was adopted by various manufacturers including Citroën, Panhard, Somua and Unic, as well as several foreign concerns. This new design was used throughout the 1930s, mainly for military vehicles, and differed from the original design in various fundamental respects. The driving axle was at the forward end and equipped with sprockets (instead of friction drive from rear-mounted axle). The new tracks featured metal cross-pieces and were of a sturdier design. The suspension, too, was redesigned.

17A

17B

16: French heavy artillery tractor by Somua, employing late type Kégresse rear bogies and fitted with hoisting gear and 'fifth wheel' coupling. Somua *(Société d'Outillage Mécanique et Usinage d'Artillerie)* was founded during the first World War to continue the automobile production side of Schneider and produced various types of semi-track vehicles as well as the very successful S-35 cavalry tank and the AMR Gendron-Somua armoured car.

17A: Another heavy Somua artillery tractor of the early 1930s, the MCL. It was used for towing 155–mm guns of the 'full-trailer' type. A smaller type, Model MCG, was also produced.
17B: Unic Model P107 artillery tractor. Like the Somuas, Unic semi-track tractors of the French Army were captured by the Germans in 1939/40 in relatively large numbers and subsequently used by the *Wehrmacht*.

18A: Citroën-Kégresse in the Gobi desert in Central Asia. This vehicle was one of seven used in the 'China Group' of the 'Yellow Expedition' which took place between April 1931 and March 1932 as an overland link between the Mediterranean and the Pacific, connecting Beirut, the French port of the Middle East, with the French colony of Indochina (now Vietnam).

18B: Citroën-Kégresse over-snow ambulance of the mid-1930s, used by the French Army.

18C: One of several types of German modifications of captured Somua-Kégresse half-tracks: *15 cm Panzerwerfer 42*. Note armoured body, not unlike that of the *Sd. Kfz. 251* APC.

18D: Somua-Kégresse model MCG 11 artillery tractor under test, pulling a 155-mm gun. This type was first introduced in about 1929 and had Kégresse type P 16 T track bogies. Engine was 4-cyl. petrol, developing

18A

18B

18C

18D

60 bhp at 2000 rpm. On the same chassis the French Army also had a recovery vehicle, which was used by the Armoured Divisions.

19A: Citroën-Kégresse (1931) belonging to Military Tractors, a subsidiary of the Artillery Transport Co. of Copmanthorpe, near York. These firms specialised in hiring vehicles out to British Territorial Army Artillery Units for their annual exercises and to Regular Army mechanised units. They had six light and twelve medium Citroën-Kégresse vehicles (tractors and staff cars), six Crossley-Kégresses, and many wheeled vehicles, notably Morris-Commercial and Karrier 6 × 4.

19B: Polish-built Fiat (Polski Fiat) model 621 L with Kégresse bogies and ambulance body, built in 1935. Artillery tractor version also produced.

19C: Burford-Kégresse model MA 3-ton chassis with cab. Used by the British Army as Field Artillery Tractor, it could carry a crew of six and 100 rounds of ammunition, and tow a field gun and limber.

19D: This Belgian Kégresse-type artillery tractor, built by FN of Herstal near Liège, was similar to the French Somua.

19A

19B

19C

19D

During the 1920s, concurrently with the Kégresse system in France, Roadless Traction Ltd, of Hounslow, England, designed various types of half-track bogie conversions for cars, trucks and traction engines. The low-pressure pneumatic tyre did not exist then and tracks were the only solution for good off-road performance. On some Roadless types the tracks could flex laterally and their rubber-jointed ones had three times the life of a pin-jointed track. Later a driven girder type was introduced and fitted in large numbers on Fordson Major tractors. During the late 1920s the firm introduced their 'Orolo' track bogie units which could take the place of driving or non-driving wheels. They were used on life boat carriages and trailers and during World War II on a 45-ton 4-track tank recovery trailer.

21B

21A

20: Foden steam tractor fitted with Roadless track bogies (circa 1924). Foden's earlier (1922) half-track load carrier 'carried a 5-ton pay load with ease over all sorts of ground negotiable by the front wheels'. A contemporary Sentinel-Roadless steam tractor could pull three 5-furrow ploughs at once or a 20-ton load.

21A: AEC model 501 (formerly 'Y'-type) 3-tonner experimentally equipped with Roadless track bogies—a conversion more frequent on light truck chassis such as Guy, Morris-Commercial and Vulcan.

21B: British FWD/Roadless half-track tractor under test, towing a 60-pounder gun. This tractor had a 4-cyl. 42-bhp engine and a driven front axle.

21C: One of many 'one-off' Morris-Commercial/Roadless half-track vehicles, fitted with attractive touring car coachwork.

21C

CHRISTIE CRAWLERS

During the 1920s the American firm of Christie Crawlers, Inc. of 156 Wilson Avenue, Newark, New Jersey (later home of the Trucktor Corp'n, six-wheeler conversion specialists) marketed various types of half-track attachments for conversion of conventional vehicles. The sales literature said: 'The secret of the high speed and long life of Christie Crawlers is the shock-absorbing effect of rubber tires, super-spring action and elimination of all small exposed wearing parts. Comparison of the Christie Crawler to all other crawlers is like comparing a truck on rubber tires to one that runs on steel wheels, without rubber tires. The Christie Crawler with its super-springs places the magic band of rubber between track and wheels. The result is a better crawler at high speed, long life and quickly convertible to rubber tires for rapid road travel.'

23A

22: This 5-ton Mack of the famous 'Bulldog' type, fitted with Christie Crawler attachment, was tested by the US Army Ordnance Department.

23A: Type T Christie Crawler on a Mack Model AB DR 2½-ton dump truck, illustrating the great width of the track. The non-skid track shoes of special heat-treated alloy steel provided 'the sure-footed traction which keeps trucks equipped with Christie Crawlers on the job every day, rain or shine'.

23B: White dump truck equipped with Type T Christie Crawler conversion. As can be seen, the additional pair of wheels was fitted in front of the original rear axle. The coil springs which kept the track under tension are also clearly visible in this illustration.

23B

AMERICAN KÉGRESSE DEVELOPMENTS

In May 1931 the US Army acquired a Citroën-Kégresse P17 half-track from France for tests and evaluation. By December of the following year the first American half-track with continuous rubber-band tracks was delivered by James Cunningham, Son & Co. of Rochester, New York. It was designated *Car, Half-Track, T1*. In 1933 Rock Island Arsenal produced 30 of an improved version, T1E1. General Motors, in 1933, produced the

Truck, Half-Track, T1. The half-track truck T2 was a Ford 1½-ton converted by Cunningham in August 1933 (but barred from production because the company failed to comply with NRA regulations). The T3 was produced by Linn (see next section), and T4 and T5 were built by GM, using Cunningham rear bogies. Some T5s were experimentally fitted with different types of tracks (T5E1, T5E2).

25A

25B

24: *Car, Half-Track, T1:* reconnaissance car produced by Cunningham in 1932. First US application of Kégresse system. Cunningham later converted Chevrolet and Ford trucks into half-tracks.
25A: *Truck, Half-Track, T1:* one-ton truck by GMC, 1933. Initial order for six was cancelled. Of the T4 model, which apart from rear body

had similar appearance, 22 were supplied in 1934 for use as wire-laying trucks by the Signal Corps.
25B: *Truck, Half-Track, T5:* designed by GMC in 1934. Twenty-four delivered in 1935 for use as artillery tractors. Like the T4 it was equipped with Cunningham rear bogies.

Development of military half-track vehicles in the USA continued throughout the 1930s. In June 1933 the first three units of a heavy type were supplied by the Linn Manufacturing Corporation of Morris, New York. These units were designated *Truck, Half-Track, T3* (Linn Model WD-12) and were powered by a 246-bhp 12-cyl. in-Vee American LaFrance engine. One of these vehicles is shown on the opposite page. It was fitted with a powerful winch, located behind the cab.

Another model was produced by Linn in 1934. This was designated *Truck, Half-Track, T6* and had the USA military registration number W-40160. It was smaller than the T3 and did not feature a winch. The Linn Mfg Corp. produced half-track trucks and tractors from about 1916. Most were similar to the Lombard tractors in that the track bogies were located on the inside of the chassis frame side members.

By the end of the 1930s another Linn company (Linn Coach and Truck Corp., Oneonta, New York) introduced a wheel-cum-track truck of unusual design. This 5-ton vehicle (Model C5) had a driven front axle and at the rear a tracked bogie as well as a suspended trailing axle. This 'dead' rear axle could be lowered hydraulically and take the load off the tracks when the vehicle was needed only for running over well-made surfaces. When the tracks were off the ground they were no longer driven and the vehicle was propelled by its front wheels only. Linn trucks and tractors were also available in Britain, sales being handled by the BMB Engineering Co., Britannia House, Ampton Street, London W.C.1. From late 1940 the company produced large front-wheel drive 12-litre metropolitan-type ambulances for the US Army. During 1946/47 Linn was reorganised to become the Linn Coach & Truck Division of Great American Industries, but it seems that the company stopped making trucks about 1953 when it was sold by Great American.

27A

26: The Linn WD-12 half-track truck weighed 25 000 lb. and had a payload capacity of 8 tons. Its towing capacity was just over 15 tons.
27A: Linn C5 wheel-cum-track chassis, 1940.
27B: Linn advertisement of 1920.

13 of the 25 Towns in Otsego County, N. Y. Own Linn Tractors

Other townships are being equipped with Linn Tractors and Trailers as fast as we can build them. Spring sees a vast amount of road work started and accomplished earlier than usual because Linn Tractors can be operated in stone fields, sand pits and other seemingly inaccessible places just as efficiently as a truck travels the built-up road.

Linn Tractors will drag the hones and haul the concrete for sluices and do almost innumerable other heavy tasks that lighten the burden and lessen the cost of road construction and maintenance.

Linn Tractors keep busy the year 'round. Oiling and watering the roads;

breaking the roads and plowing the snow in winter; hauling milk, lumber, coal and chemical wood — these are a few of the many daily uses of Linn Tractors. They welcome the trial with trucks or teams that will determine comparative costs. On long trips, with heavy loads, through hard going, Linn Tractors often do the work at half the cost.

We will gladly give details concerning the possibilities with Linn Tractors in your territory. Immediate correspondence is urged, for right now there exists in many localities a tremendous potential market.

Linn Manufacturing Corporation
Morris, N. Y.

LINN
GEARED TO THE GROUND
TRACTOR

Showing the *flexible* lag-bed of the Linn Tractor in action. Note the ground gain over the *rigid* type of traction member. Over ruts and rises, the entire length of the lag-bed hugs the ground.

In July 1936 the Marmon-Herrington Company of Indianapolis, Indiana, produced a half-track truck for the US Ordnance Department, designated T9. It consisted of a regular 1936 Ford V8 1½-ton truck chassis, fitted with M.-H. front axle drive conversion and Kégresse-type bogies. It performed remarkably well, owing partly to its driving front axle, and set new standards for this type of vehicle for military service. The T8 was also a commercial Ford Truck, converted into a half-track by the use of a Trackson attachment (see page 58). One T9 was reconverted experimentally in 1937 and fitted with two-wheel bogies (T9E1). Also in that year two more Fords were converted, now of the 1937 model year. This became the Ford/Marmon-Herrington. *Truck, Half-Track, M2.*

29A

28: This 1936 Ford truck was converted into a half-track truck by Marmon-Herrington and was one of the first of its type with driven front axle. The unit shown had two-wheel track bogies and was designated *Truck, Half-Track, T9E1.*
29A: The final model in the series of Ford/Marmon-Herrington T9 half-track trucks was this unit which was standardised as *Truck, Half-Track, M2.* It was produced in 1937 and based on the 1937 Ford 1½-ton truck.
29B: Believed to be the last-ever half-track vehicle produced by Marmon-Herrington was the armoured model DHT-5 of 1941/42, which was probably a conversion of the earlier 4 × 4 armoured car, T11. It had a 37-mm gun mounted in a revolving turret and the engine was at the rear.

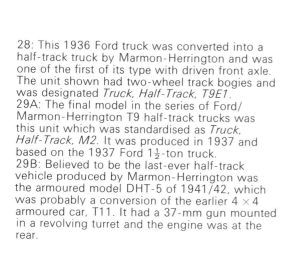

29B

During the late 1920s the German Army began to show an interest in off-road tractors for various purposes and by 1932 a family of semi-track vehicles of various sizes was scheduled, incorporating Richter track bogies. For every size one firm was selected to carry out the design and development work. Other firms were to be engaged on boosting production if necessary. The following types were envisaged:

1-ton (towed load) *Sd.Kfz.10* (Demag), 3–ton *Sd.Kfz.11* (Hansa-Lloyd), 5-ton *Sd.Kfz.6* (Büssing-NAG), 8-ton *Sd.Kfz.7* (Krauss-Maffei), 12-ton *Sd.Kfz.8* (Daimler-Benz), 18-ton *Sd.Kfz.9* (Famo).

These were later supplemented by the *Sd.Kfz.2 Kettenkrad* (NSU) and many derivations based on the standardised types. Shown here are some of the early models in the medium and heavy series.

31B

31A

31C

30: One of the factory halls of Krauss-Maffei at Allach near Munich, about 1937. The chassis in the fore- and background are of the medium KM m 11 type (8-ton *Sd.Kfz.7*, as produced from 1937–45); on the left are several of the earlier KM m 8 vehicles, fitted with artillery tractor and truck type bodywork. During 1935–37 Krauss-Maffei built 380 KM m 8, 257 KM m 9 and 111 KM m 10 vehicles.

31A: The first Daimler-Benz heavy semi-track tractor, Model ZD5, was produced in 1931. It was very different from the later standardised models. Front and rear suspension were interconnected.

31B: One of the first production types: the medium Krauss-Maffei KM m 8 of 1934/35, shown with early type bodywork.

31C: Daimler-Benz model DB s 7 units of 1934/5 on parade in Nürnberg towing heavy artillery.

KETTENKRAD

The smallest of the German semi-track vehicles of World War II, the NSU-built Opel-powered *Kleines Kettenkraftrad* (small tracked motor cycle), *Sd.Kfz.2*, usually referred to as *Kettenkrad*, made its debut in the invasion of Crete in 1941 and was used in North Africa and on the Eastern and Western Front. Only a few are left today. The 4-cyl. Opel Olympia 1.5-litre ohv engine was located centrally, back-to-front, driving the front sprockets through a six-speed transmission. The front wheel steered the vehicle through slight bends but when the handlebars were turned more than a certain angle the steering brakes (controlled differential) came into action for sharp turns.

33A

33B

32: Rare crane version of the *Kettenkrad*. (Inset shows a prototype.)
33A: The *NSU-Kettenkrad* was used for various purposes, namely as a transporter for troops and supplies (often with special two-wheel trailer), signals vehicle, wire-laying vehicle (special versions *Sd.Kfz. 2/1 Kl.K. Krad für Feldfernkabel* and *Sd.Kfz. 2/2 Kl.K.Krad für schweres Fernkabel)*, lumber tractor, anti-tank gun tractor etc.

33B: In the Karelian forests the *Kettenkrad* was used as a lumber tractor. In low gear and low transfer the overall gear ratio (incl. final drives) was 68.59:1; in top gear high range it was 4.23:1. Top speed was 80 km/h; normal cruising speed at 3000 engine rpm was 61.5 km/h or about 40 mph. Without trailer the machine could climb a 24° incline.

C

The German light semi-track *Zgkw (Zugkraftwagen)* series consisted of the 1-ton and 3-ton ranges. Parent firm of the 1-tonner was Demag AG of Wetter/Ruhr and there were unarmoured, partially and fully armoured models. The same applied to the somewhat larger 3-ton models, parent firm of which was Hansa-Lloyd (later Borgward). Except for early production all models had 6-cyl. Maybach engines. Starting in 1937 the Adler-Werke AG in Frankfurt/Main developed a range of vehicles similar in concept to the Demag series. This series, designated HK 300 (HK = *Halbketten* = half-track), included a passenger car (HK300/A3F), but their development ceased in 1941. In 1942 Adler started development of a much-simplified semi-track vehicle: the *le WS (leichter Wehrmachts-*

schlepper = light military tractor), intended to supersede the sophisticated Demag types. Some prototypes were produced but all development was cancelled in 1944.

The first vehicle in the 3-ton series was built in 1934 and had a Hansa-Lloyd-Goliath engine. Soon afterwards some rear-engined prototypes were produced, intended for armoured bodywork. The armoured version to enter mass-production, however, was the front-engined Hanomag H kl 6p which bore the designation *Sd.Kfz.251*, and appeared in many variations. Except for the armoured hull it was very similar to the 'soft-skin' *Sd.Kfz.11* series which also appeared in various forms, including artillery tractors and coast guard ambulances.

35A

35B

35C

35D

34: One of more than twenty variations of armoured vehicles in the German *Sd.Kfz.251* range.

35A: This light semi-track tractor, D 11 2, was one of the first Demag-built prototypes for the 1-ton series. The engine, a 6-cyl. BMW 315, was mounted back-to-front at the rear.

35B: *Sd.Kfz.* 10 1-ton prime movers (Demag D7) during the occupation of Amsterdam in May 1940. Note the Dutch policemen helplessly

watching the invaders go by.

35C: The partially armoured *Sd.Kfz.251/17* mounted a *2 cm Flak 36* anti-aircraft gun. It was a comparatively rare model.

35D: During 1937–38 Daimler-Benz marketed this commercial semi-track *'Zwitter'* truck, model LR75. It had a petrol engine and would climb gradients of up to 50°

The medium types of German semi-track tractors were the *Sd.Kfz.6* (5-ton) and *Sd.Kfz.7* (8-ton) series. Parent firm for the *Sd.Kfz.6* was Büssing-NAG, for the *Sd.Kfz.7* Krauss-Maffei. Several other firms were also engaged in their production, including Praga in Czechoslovakia and Saurer in Austria. Large numbers were produced. Krauss-Maffei alone, by 1943, produced 100 8-ton model KM m 11 vehicles per month. From 1937 until their factories near Munich were occupied in 1945 this firm delivered no fewer than 5026 of these machines. In addition, Krauss-Maffei produced another 30 for the British occupation forces during Sept.–Oct. 1945, and 315 heavy 12-ton types (DB 10) during 1940–41. Borgward also produced considerable quantities of the 8-ton type (model HL m 11).

37A

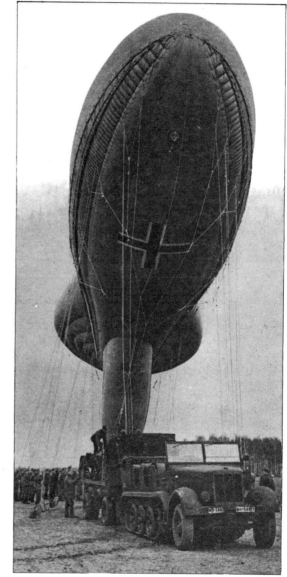

36: *Sd.Kfz.6* Semi-track Engineers: tractor for 5-ton towed loads, produced by Büssing-NAG. The *Sd.Kfz.6/1* Artillery version featured the usual ammunition compartment at the rear. Both had a 100-bhp Maybach engine and eight forward gears. Crew 15 and 11 respectively.
37A: Krauss-Maffei 8-ton tractor, fitted with unusual wooden truck-type bodywork, photographed with German Army unit in the Oder sector in March 1945. From 1935 to 1945 Krauss-Maffei produced a total of 6129 semi-track vehicles, mainly for the *Wehrmacht*.
37B: Trailer with cable balloon, used for observation purposes, towed by *Sd.Kfz.7* 8-ton tractor. Maximum road speed of this model was 55 km/h.

37B

38: The *Wehrmacht's* family of semi-track tractors in 1939. Left to right: 1-ton (Demag), 3-ton (Hanomag), 5-ton (Büssing-NAG), 8-ton (Krauss-Maffei), 12-ton (Daimler-Benz), 18-ton (Famo). The latter is shown here with the rare artillery tractor bodywork.
39A: Heavy 12-ton semi-track *Sd.Kfz.8* (Daimler-Benz, model DB s 8) under test, towing four-wheel gun carriage.
39B: Typical German advertising of the period.

39C: Famo 18-ton *schwerer Zugkraftwagen (Sd.Kfz.9)* being reversed on to its tracks. These tracks, similar except for size on all German *Zgkw.*, featured needle roller bearings and detachable rubber track pads.
39D: Applying the grease gun to every one of the track links was a time-consuming task and was easier at the works than in the field. Note winch cable and king-size towing attachment.

39A

39C

39D

MERCEDES-BENZ

39B

The German standardised semi-track designs were copied in several other countries. The Swedish Volvo (Fig. 40A) was built during the war and was very similar to the German 1-ton *Sd.Kfz.10* (Demag). The Czech OT810 (Fig. 40D) was produced after the war and resembled the APC *Sd.Kfz.251* but was powered by a Tatra V8 engine. The Czechoslovakian forces, after 1945, used left-overs of most of the German WWII types including a crane version similar to the Famo 18-ton *Sd.Kfz.9/1*, but based on the Krauss-Maffei 8-ton *Sd.Kfz.7*. It was used by the Czech Air Force on airfields.

The Italian Fiat 727 SC (*Semicingolato* = semi-track) was first conceived in 1941 and featured track bogies of the German Richter design. After the prototype (Fig. 40B) was produced and tested in 1943, approval was given for its production, to start in April 1944. This, however, never materialised.

40A

40B

40C

40D

The vehicle weighed less than 3½ tons and had a drawbar pull of 6 tons. Payload capacity was 1½ tons at a speed of 53 km/h. Fiat also produced semi-track versions of the Spa 'Dovunque' cross-country truck.

The Italian Breda (Fig. 40C) was patterned on the German 8-ton *Sd.Kfz.7*. It would appear that a few hundred were produced for the German Army in 1944. It had a 140-bhp Breda T14 petrol engine. Finally there was the British 'Traclat', half a dozen of which were produced in 1944/45 by Vauxhall Motors (Model BT: Bedford Tractor; Figures 41 A/B/C). Shown are a scale-model, the prototype under test and one that was used after the war as a lumber tractor. The 'Traclat' was patterned on the German *Sd.Kfz.7* but was powered by twin Bedford truck engines. Tests were successful but the cessation of the war caused the end of this development.

41A

41B

41C

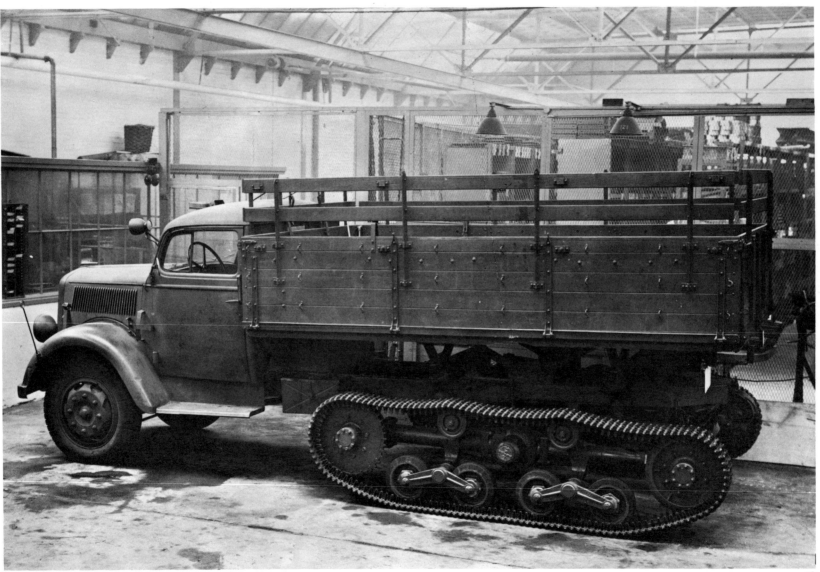

MAULTIER

With the *Blitzkrieg* advances into Russia in 1941/42 it soon became apparent that the common 4×2 conventional type trucks (Borgward, Ford, Mercedes-Benz, Opel etc.) were virtually useless in negotiating the extremely muddy terrain where proper roads were usually non-existent. There being no time to wait for sufficient supply of all-wheel drive vehicles, the *Wehrmacht* started employing ordinary trucks converted into semi-track vehicles. These vehicles, known as *Maultier* (Mule), were subsequently produced by various firms, using standard Ford, Klöckner (KHD), and Opel chassis. Several kinds of bogies and tracks were used, the most common being those of the British Carden-Loyd type.

Various experiments were carried out with different types such as the Opel Blitz shown opposite which was converted in occupied Holland. Except for the Mercedes-Benz all were originally 3-tonners but after conversion the official payload capacity was derated to 2-tons. The Ford and the Opel were the most numerous, but as load carriers the least satisfactory because of their high-speed petrol engines which were not suited for slow-moving semi-track vehicles, the maximum permissible speed of which was only 16 km/h (10 mph). In this respect the Klöckner-Humboldt-Deutz version with its low-speed Deutz diesel engine was the most successful vehicle. Of the Opel *Maultier* there were also armoured versions, mainly as mobile rocket-launchers. The Mercedes-Benz 4½-tonner semi-track was devised mainly as a stop-gap when it was decided to stop production of the 5-ton *Sd.Kfz.6* and replace it with the *schwerer Wehrmachtsschlepper* (see next page).

43A

43B

43C

42: Experimental *Maultier* (Mule) semi-track conversion of the standard German Army Opel Blitz 3-ton 4 × 2 truck. This model did not go into series production.

43A: Several hundred Opels were fitted with armoured bodywork and 15-cm multiple rocket-launching devices. Designated *Panzerwerfer 42,* and firing the same rockets as the *15-cm Nebelwerfer,* this equipment was successfully used by *Panzergrenadier* units, especially on the Western front.

43B: Many *Maultier* vehicles saw service on the Eastern Front. On the right is a Famo 18-ton *Sd.Kfz.9.*

43C: The Mercedes-Benz L4500R had a diesel engine and light tank (*Panzer II*) track bogies. Also appeared as Wrecker.

LIGHT AND HEAVY MILITARY TRACTORS

The standardised family of German semi-track vehicles was ingenious, successful and most impressive but also costly in production and upkeep. By 1942 the High Command of the *Wehrmacht* decided to introduce two new types of semi-track vehicles with much-simplified dry-pin track bogies. The heaviest of the two was called *schwerer Wehrmachtsschlepper (sWS)* and was introduced as a replacement for both the 5-ton *Sd.Kfz.6* and the makeshift *Maultier*. Production was undertaken by Büssing-NAG and Tatra, and started towards the end of 1943. It took a long time before production was in full swing and as an interim solution the Mercedes-Benz L4500R *Maultier* was produced (see previous section). By the time the war ended only relatively few *sWS* had been produced. The *sWS* appeared in various forms, namely cargo carrier, armoured rocket-launcher and partially armoured SP mount for anti-aircraft gun *(37 mm Flak 43)*. In 1953 Tatra in Czechoslovakia modified a *sWS* and fitted it with their V-12 air-cooled diesel engine. This became the prototype for the Tatra T809 of 1955, which, however, did not go into quantity production. Even fewer were produced of the *leichter Wehrmachtsschlepper (leWS)*. This type was developed by Adler during 1942–44 and was intended as a simplified replacement for the lighter *Zgkw.* types, mainly the 1-ton *Sd.Kfz.10*.

45A

45B

44: Heavy military tractor (*sWS*-*schwerer Wehrmachtsschlepper*) as produced by Büssing-NAG and Tatra to a common *Wehrmacht* specification. Visible in the cargo body of this Tatra-built unit is a complete armoured front end with cab shell which was fitted on certain models.
45A: Tatra produced this development of the *sWS*, now designated

T809, in 1955. It was powered by a 140-bhp air-cooled V-8 diesel engine of almost 10 litres cubic capacity. It had a payload of 8 tons and a track ground pressure of 0.6 kg/cm².
45B: The second pilot model for the light military tractor (*le WS*-*leichter Wehrmachtsschlepper*), produced by Adler of Frankfurt/Main late in 1942. Like the *sWS* it featured simplified track bogies with dry link pins.

Towards the end of the 1930s the Americans had finalised the development of their Kégresse-type half-track bogies and early in 1939 a half-track
modification of the US Cavalry's scout car made its appearance at the
Rock Island Arsenal. It was designated T7 and was the progenitor of the
Car, Half-Track, M2 and the slightly longer *Carrier, Personnel, Half-Track,
M3*. These two APCs, with seating capacity of 10 and 13 respectively,
were subsequently produced in large numbers by Autocar, Diamond T
and White and also formed the basis for countless standardised and
experimental modifications such as mortar carriers and SP gun mounts.

47A

46: Typical example of American half-track vehicle of World War II.
Shown is an early 81-mm mortar carrier, M4, which was similar
externally to the half-track car, M2. US half-track vehicles of various
types were used by the American and Allied forces, including the Soviet
Union, in enormous quantities, and large numbers are still in military
and commercial use all over the world.
47A: The prototype of the US half-track was a combination of the scout
car, M3, and the half-track truck, M2. Rear axle and drive sprockets on
this model were at the rear end of the track bogies.
47B: Two generations of US armoured personnel carriers: the half-
tracked M3 of 1940 and the full-tracked M113 of 1960.

47B

48A: Top view of a 'tank chaser', armed with what was basically the famous French 75-mm gun of WWI. This vehicle, officially known as *Carriage, Motor, 75-mm Gun, T12*, was developed at APG (Aberdeen Proving Ground) on a modified M3 half-track APC and was the first self-propelled gun adopted by the US Army in WWII.

48B: The 105-mm howitzer carriage, T19, of 1941. Early production half-tracks all had truck-type 'drop-centre' front wheels and a roller at the front to prevent rooting in ditches or against steep banks and to facilitate going through brush and small trees. Later models had combat-type wheels and in most cases a 5-ton power winch at front. Later production also had the stalk-mounted headlight units, as standardised for all US AFVs.

48C: The standardised version of the 75-mm gun motor carriage, T12 (shown on left), was this M3 model which featured larger gun shields and other improvements. A number of these, produced by Autocar, saw active service in the Pacific area, notably the Philippines, in 1941/42.

48A

48B

48C

49A: One of many motorised gun mounts designed and developed at Aberdeen Proving Ground during World War II was this experimental *Carriage, Motor, Multiple Gun, T68*. It was armed with twin Bofors guns with 'equilibrator' elevation adjustment device.

49B: Artist's impression of 'streamlined' half-track APC with fully sloping armour. Project only.

49C: Pre-production US Army Cavalry half-track scout car, featuring different track bogies with drive to the rear sprockets. On the series-produced models these sprockets were at the forward ends of the bogies and the idler wheels (which were adjustable for track tension adjustment) at the rear.

49D: The T16 half-track truck (Diamond T) was larger than the standardised types although it resembled them in several respects. Track bogies and body were considerably longer but because of the shorter front end the overall length was only 5 in. more. Other armoured half-track trucks were the T17 (Autocar, White) and T19 (Mack) but none were produced in quantity.

49A

49B

49C

49D

The requirements for half-track vehicles by the US Army and its Allies, particularly Canada, Great Britain and Russia, were such that another supplier was needed and this is where the International Harvester Co. of Chicago came into the picture. Some standardised models, M2 and M3, were experimentally fitted with the International 'Red Diamond' engine and other components (M2E5 and M3E2 respectively) and these were the prototypes for a new range of IHC-built half-track vehicles, consisting of the M5, M9 and M14 series. They were similar in design to the standard models but there were many distinguishing features, such as IHC banjo-type front axle, flat-section wings, welded hull with rounded rear corners, different dashboard etc.

50: British Army half-track vehicle in difficulties. Originally this was a gun motor carriage, M14, 1600 of which were supplied to the British who converted them into trucks, personnel carriers and command vehicles (shown). They remained in use for many years.

51A: IHC half-track personnel carrier M5 or M9, which were identical in external appearance, in French Army service. M5A1 and M9A1 had an armoured ringmount ('pulpit') above the front passenger seat. Note added early type headlights.

51B: International multiple gun motor carriage, M14, in its original form Note hinged side top panels.

51C: British Army post-war radar vehicle conversion of APC M5 or M9. The British usually removed the front roller (if vehicle was thus equipped). Vehicle tows a 1-ton 2-wheel generator trailer.

51B

51A

51C

US WARTIME PRODUCTION

The standardised family of half-track vehicles produced in the United States during World War II proved quite successful and large numbers were turned out by the Autocar Co. in Ardmore, Pennsylvania, the Diamond T Motor Co. in Chicago, Illinois, and the White Motor Co. in Cleveland, Ohio. Mechanically all the standard models were identical, featuring a White model 160 AX 6-cyl. side-valve petrol engine developing 147 bhp at 3000 rpm, a Spicer gearbox-cum-transfer providing 4×2 forward gears, Timken-Detroit driving axles (split-type at front, banjo-type rear), Bendix-Wagner hydraulic brakes with hydrovac power assistance, Timken-Detroit track bogies with cable-reinforced rubber tracks. Except for the axles most chassis components, including the rear bogie, were identical on the IHC-built models.

53A

Part way down the Half-Track assembly line, illustrating the rear bogie construction and the driving tracks

53B

53D

Armor-plate is unyielding and very heavy—mounting the body calls for exact workmanship, close attention

53C

52: Early White-built half-track cars, M2, taking part in manoeuvres in the United States in 1941. Also shown are a 1941 Plymouth sedan, a ½-ton 4 × 4 Dodge and a 1½-ton 4 × 4 Chevrolet.

53A: Half-track chassis assembly line of the Diamond T Motor Car Co. in Chicago.

53B: Further down the assembly line, showing in the foreground the chassis for the 245th 57-mm gun motor carriage, T48.

53C: The face-hardened ¼-in. armour plate panels were bolted on to a framework and the complete rear body assembly is here seen being lowered on to the chassis. Armour-plate scuttle and bonnet (hood) are already bolted in position.

53D: Three-quarter rear view of an APC M3. By comparison, the International-built M5 and M9 models had a welded body with rounded rear quarters and bumperettes.

54A: US Army vehicles roll through the streets of Colmar, France, following that city's liberation. Leading vehicles are multiple gun motor carriages, M16, also known as 'Wippers'. They had four 0.50 cal. machine guns and were originally designated T58. Later developed into M16A1 and M16A2, featuring armoured shields for the guns and full-height body sides.

54B: Half-track personnel carriers, M3A1, of the Ninth US Army advance on a German road east of the river Roer following the crossing of the river on 23rd February 1945. (A week later, 2nd March, the Ninth Army reached the west bank of the Rhine).

54C: These modified half-tracks were used in US Army manoeuvres in Alaska in 1946/47. Modifications were many and included fitting of a truck-type cargo body, hard-top cab and dual front wheels with track chains.

54A

54B

54C

55A: Vehicles of the First US Army's Third Armoured Division in street of war-wrecked Pulheim, Germany, during the drive towards Cologne in March 1945. Vehicles shown: half-track APC, M3A1, with ¾-ton 2-wheeled cargo trailer, GMC 2½-ton 6 × 6 cargo truck, and Dodge ¾-ton 4 × 4 'Beep'.
55B: Wireless vehicle of the post-war British Army, based on half-track APC M3. The trailer is a wartime *Trailer, 10-cwt, 2-wh., G.S., No. 1.*

55C: Much more numerous in the British Army were the International Harvester half-track APCs M5, M9 etc. The M14 multiple gun motor carriages in British WD service were modified by demounting the guns and adding seats to fill a Personnel role, roughly equivalent to that of the APC M9. Others were fitted with an A-frame type crane on the front bumper and used by the REME. Shown here is one of various types.

55A

55B

55C

56A: Interior view of the International Harvester-produced APC M5A1 with seating for 13, including driver. Armoured machine gun ring mount and rifle scabbard mounts can be seen clearly. Big problem with these APCs was shortage of storage space for crew members' kit and belongings.

56B: APC M5A1 (IHC) of post-war Dutch Army.

56C: Another type of British Army REME repair vehicle based on IHC-built half-track vehicle. Sheerlegs on front bumper enabled crew to replace tank power units etc. in the field. Comprehensive array of tools and equipment was carried.

56D: Half-track-based mobile crane with a difference. The rear end is familiar; the front end is ex-AEC 'Matador' truck with diesel engine. Joined up amidships this hybrid civilian vehicle saw many years of service in the south of England and still exists.

56A

56B

56C

56D

57A: Half-track APC, M3A1, of the Dutch Army, circa 1960. As an APC the military half-track in the Netherlands was superseded by the multi-wheeled (8 × 6) DAF YP-408.

57B: Large numbers of various types of ex-WW II American half-track vehicles are still in use in the Israeli Army. Having fitted it with a simple sextant for desert navigation and some other detail modifications, the Israelis have proved that after 25 years the US half-track is still a sound and very useful combat vehicle.

57C: M16 half-track SPs were among the vehicles supplied by the United States to the post-war armies of Germany, Japan (shown) and others.

57D: Thousands of war-surplus half-track vehicles, new or used, found their way into civilian life and were employed for various peaceful purposes. This is a dump trunk conversion marketed during the 1950s by Tunick Brothers of Stamford, Connecticut, USA.

57A

57B

57C

57D

The easiest way to produce a half-track vehicle was to fit so-called overall chains round the rear wheels of a six-wheeled vehicle and several examples of this type are shown on this page. The most successful applications were those on vehicles where the rear wheels moved only in a vertical plane, as for example on the Scammell 'Pioneer' and DAF Trado. The advantages here were that the wheels within the track always remained in the same position relative to each other and at the same distance from each other. As a result it was not necessary for the track to 'twist' and to absorb bogie wheelbase variations when negotiating rough terrain.

58B

58A

58C

58A: This Model AA Ford truck of 1929 vintage was converted by the firm of SYS N.V. (later, Netam) of Schiedam, Netherlands, during the early 1930s. The rear bogie arrangement and the overall chains can be seen clearly. Load carried and towed (a dozen men and a heavy gun) seems excessive. System was perfected by Messrs. van der Trappen and van Doorne (of DAF) as the TRADO system and successfully used on Chevrolet, Ford, GMC, and other trucks.

58B: The famed British Scammell heavy breakdown tractor was an ideal vehicle to convert into a half-track and as such would go anywhere.

58C: Trackson of Milwaukee marketed this cable and chain half-track conversion kit for commercial trucks. Fitted on a 1935/36 Ford the US Army tested it as *Truck, Half-Track, T8.*

When Adolphe Kégresse set out to improve the over-snow performance of the cars belonging to his employer, Czar Nicholas II of Russia, he replaced the driven rear wheels by long flexible tracked bogies and provided for skis to replace (or fit under) the front wheels. This system proved most successful and was subsequently used in various countries. Obviously the wider the tracks the lower the ground pressure and dual wheels were often used to enable the use of wider tracks. The system was also used for full-track (non-convertible) vehicles, especially in Canada where many vehicles have been built with dual truck wheels with pneumatic tyres incorporated in bogies with very wide tracks. Such snow and mud vehicles are still in production and have been perfected to a high degree.

59B

59A

59C

59A: 1937 Ford bus-cum-load carrier operated in Finland for over-snow transportation. Skis were added to the front wheels.
59B: Czechoslovakian Tatra T71 half-track over-snow vehicle produced in 1932. It was an experimental conversion of the firm's 6 × 4 light truck, featuring a 4-cyl. horizontally opposed 1910-cc air-cooled engine, built in unit with transmission and tubular chassis backbone in which the drive line was encased (design Ledwinka). An auxiliary gearbox was fitted to provide a high and low range of gear ratios (4F1R × 2).
59C: Allis-Chalmers over-snow tractor, M7, produced during World War II for the US forces. The vehicle had two seats, one behind the other, and had many parts in common with the standardised ¼-ton 4 × 4 'Jeep', including the complete engine/transmission assembly.

60A: Half-track conversion of a 1932 Peugeot 201C two-seater car. Note all-enclosed bogie suspension and endless band-type front roller.

60B: Experimental half-track produced by the Danish firm of Forenede Automobil Fabriken A.S. in Odense, under the trade name Triangel. The bogie incorporated the truck's original rear axle and wheels and the track is of the endless rubber band type. Triangel was the only truck of any importance built in Denmark between the first and second World War (1918–1940).

60C: The French Somua firm was actively engaged during the 1930s on the production of various types of half-track vehicles (see pages 16–18). This is a low-silhouette type artillery tractor with space for a crew of six including the driver and ammunition lockers at rear.

60D: Another low-silhouette half-track gun tractor of French origin was this Unic model TU1. It was used in some numbers by Rommel's *Afrika Korps*. Note very low driver's position.

60A

60B

60C

60D

61A

MISCELLANEOUS MODELS

61A: During the mid-1920s some peculiar half-track one-man tanks made their appearance in Britain. They were the brain child of Major G. le Q. Martel, who built the first prototype in his own private garage in 1925. It had Morris mechanical components and Roadless Traction track bogies and was known as the Morris-Martel. The Crossley-Martel featured Kégresse bogies, but was similar in general design.

61B: The Morris-Martel during early tests. The vehicle reportedly wobbled badly at speeds in excess of 15 mph. The tail wheels were kept in contact with the ground by heavy leaf springs.

61C: Post-Kégresse Russia produced various types of half-track vehicles based on their regular GAZ and ZIS trucks. Shown here is the ZIS-42 which was in production and use during World War II.

61B

61C

62A: Following successes with double-drive bogies on trucks the British RASC in about 1927 developed some three-wheeled motor cycles. A Triumph-based model (shown) survived and is now in a military museum.

62B: 'Sno-go' conversion kit for motor cycles, developed in 1966 in the USA, shown here on a British Triumph 200-cc 'Tiger Cub'.

62C: American Tuscan half-track motor cycle produced in Salt Lake City, Utah, 1967. A two-stroke 20 HP engine drives the bogie through a four-speed gearbox and provides gradability of up to 100% (45°). Traction area 85 sq. in.

62A

62B

62C

63A: Four-track conversion of the British Land-Rover, designed around 1960 by the firm of Cuthbertson, was intended for use in swampy areas. The conversion exists of a special oscillating undercarriage with four bogies, incorporating four pneumatic-tyred wheels each and 12-in. wide tracks, riveted on to nylon/cotton reinforced rubber belts. The drive sprockets are simply bolted on to the vehicle's wheel hubs. Steering is in the conventional manner but power assistance is added. The vehicle may be converted back to normal after removing the sprockets and lifting if off the undercarriage.

63B

63C

63A

63B: The Oanes Carrier, marketed by Graham Engineering Co. Ltd in London, is usually powered by a diesel engine and can be supplied with a very wide range of special bodies, cabs and equipment. The unit shown here is fitted with a Bedford RL-type cab with RHD and during extensive tests proved capable of carrying loads of twice its own weight. These vehicles are assembled from new and rebuilt components, including many of International Harvester origin.
63C: Oanes Carrier fitted out as a mobile revolving crane by T. T. Boughton & Sons Ltd. Boom elevation, jib extension, and outriggers of this versatile go-anywhere crane are operated hydraulically.

INDEX

ACKNOWLEDGEMENTS

For the various photographs in this book, credit is hereby given to the following sources: Deutsches Museum, E. C. Armées, Icks Collection, Imperial War Museum, Murray Collection, US Army, Vanderveen Collection.